# Columbia University

# Contributions to Education

## Teachers College Series

# No. 292

## AMS PRESS
### NEW YORK

# LEARNING OF BRIGHT AND DULL CHILDREN

BY

FRANK THOMPSON WILSON, Ph.D.

TEACHERS COLLEGE, COLUMBIA UNIVERSITY
CONTRIBUTIONS TO EDUCATION, No. 292

BUREAU OF PUBLICATIONS
Teachers College, Columbia University
NEW YORK CITY
1928

**Library of Congress Cataloging in Publication Data**

Wilson, Frank Thompson, 1887-
    Learning of bright and dull children.

    Reprint of the 1928 ed., issued in series:  Teachers
College, Columbia University.  Contributions to edu-
cation, no. 292.
    Originally presented as the author's thesis, Columbia.
    Bibliography:  p.
    1.  Learning ability.  2.  Exceptional children--
Education.  I.  Title.  II.  Series:  Columbia Uni-
versity.  Teachers College.  Contributions to education,
no. 292.
LB1134.W5  1972 __  371.9'2'019  77-177631
ISBN 0-404-55292-7

Reprinted by Special Arrangement with Teachers
College Press, New York, New York

From the edition of 1928, New York
First AMS edition published in 1972
Manufactured in the United States

AMS PRESS, INC.
NEW YORK, N. Y.  10003

## ACKNOWLEDGMENTS

Acknowledgments of aid and coöperation are due to a great many more persons than can be named, who, by encouraging and helpful words, by much personal inconvenience and some annoyance, cheerfully made possible the gathering of the material upon which the study is based. In particular the Superintendent of the Hebrew Orphan Asylum of New York City, Mr. Lionel Simmons, and his efficient staff, and the teachers and officers in School 38 in Buffalo, and those in the practice school of the State Teachers College at Buffalo, are given the heartiest thanks of the writer. Dr. Arthur L. Gates, Dr. Rudolf Pintner, Dr. William C. Bagley, and especially Dr. L. S. Hollingworth, of Teachers College, gave invaluable advice and suggestion in the organization of the experimental work and the composition of the report. Needless to say, the more than 75 boys and girls each of whom spent an hour a day for a week in performance of the learning tasks, deserve the final award of credit for individually contributing the data upon which this study rests.

# CONTENTS

# LEARNING OF
# BRIGHT AND DULL CHILDREN

## CHAPTER I

### PURPOSE OF THE STUDY

The purpose of this study is to make a comparison of progress in learning identical novel tasks by four groups of children of selected mental abilities and chronological ages. In order to provide a probable difference in brightness, certain children were selected whose intelligence quotients by the Stanford Revision of the Binet-Simon Test fell either between 78 and 91 for the dull group, or between 109 and 122 for the bright group. It is not likely that any in either group really belong in the other group, although the true differences may not be those shown by the I.Q. figures. In order to make certain a difference in chronological age, children whose ages were within a few months of nine years were selected for the young group, and others whose ages were within a few months of twelve years were chosen for the older group.

The following questions were studied in relation to the data of this experiment:

Are there distinctive differences of kind in the learning characteristics of such groups?

Are there distinctive differences of degree in any learning characteristics which may be common to such groups?

Is ability to learn a common factor affecting all the learning of these individuals in relatively equal measure?

# CHAPTER II

## MATERIALS

### THE SUBJECTS

The data forming the basis of this report were obtained from the performance of sixty subjects, fifteen in each of four groups.[1] Chronological age was verified by both school record and children's report. The Binet test was given by the writer in the case of all children except those from the Hebrew Orphan Asylum, where this test is given by a psychologist on the staff of the institution. Through the courtesy of the superintendent, Mr. Lionel Simmons, the ratings on record there were used for the children selected from the Asylum.

The facts in the following tables are summarized from the detailed tables:

TABLE 1
DISTRIBUTION OF SUBJECTS

|  | Boys |  | Girls |  | Total |
|---|---|---|---|---|---|
| Dull 9 ..................... | 8 |  | 7 |  | 15 |
| Bright 9 ................... |  | 6 |  | 9 | 15 |
| Dull 12 .................... | 8 |  | 7 |  | 15 |
| Bright 12 ................. |  | 7 |  | 8 | 15 |
| Total Dull ............... | 16 |  | 14 |  | 30 |
| Total Bright .............. |  | 13 |  | 17 | 30 |
| Total ................. | 29 |  | 31 |  | 60 |

The children were drawn from three schools: The Hebrew Orphan Asylum, New York City; School 38, and the Normal Practice School, Buffalo, N. Y. Table 2 shows their school distribution by groups.

[1] Tables describing these data in detail have been omitted in the publication of this study, but they are on file in the office of the registrar of Teachers College, Columbia University, and may be found there.

TABLE 2
SCHOOL DISTRIBUTION OF SUBJECTS

|  |  | H.O.A. | School 38 | Practice School | Total |
|---|---|---|---|---|---|
| Dull | 9 | 9 | 6 | .. | 15 |
| Bright | 9 | 3 | 6 | 6 | 15 |
| Dull | 12 | 2 | 12 | 1 | 15 |
| Bright | 12 | 4 | 8 | 3 | 15 |
| Total | | 18 | 32 | 10 | 60 |

While this distribution may not be ideal, in that each group is not equally represented by each school, yet it is believed that effects of special local factors are materially lessened by these school and city differences among the subjects.

Table 3 gives the average I.Q.'s and M.A.'s and C.A.'s.

TABLE 3
AVERAGE I.Q.'S AND AGES OF SUBJECTS

|  |  | I.Q. | M.A. | C.A. |
|---|---|---|---|---|
| Dull | 9 | 85.1 | 7– 9 | 9– 1 |
| Bright | 9 | 114.0 | 10– 5 | 9– 2 |
| Dull | 12 | 85.0 | 10– 4 | 12– 2 |
| Bright | 12 | 115.0 | 13–11 | 12– 2 |

The data [2] show that all nine-year-old children were within at least 5 months of the same age, the range being from 8–11 to 9–4. The twelve-year-old children were likewise within 5 months of the same age, the range being from 12–0 to 12–5.

*Attitude of the Subjects.* Definite dislike for the work—or the experimenter—was shown in the case of only one child among more than 75 started on the series. This one was a twelve-year-old girl of the dull group. She daily assured the experimenter of her dislike for the work, yet she needed no particular coaxing or urging to go through the daily practices and, as a matter of fact, showed considerable interest in her results. As only four days' work was completed by this subject, however, her record does not enter into the results reported in this study. Those children who gave time outside of school hours were paid a small sum of money, five cents a day. Either the income, or the work, or the combination was sufficient to secure their regular appearance, usually well in advance of the hour set, and their

[2] Not reproduced here. See note on page 2.

willing presence until the wage was handed over. In other cases, children were excused from classes for the work, an arrangement reported to have been considered something of a distinction, possibly a welcome change, and quite the envy of other members of the class.

In the case of older children, especially the bright group, a certain degree of ennui may have developed the last day or two, at least for some of the tasks. Apparently this was the case with the reproduction, and it further seemed to the writer that this task was much less appealing to the older boys than to the older girls. Content of the selection might account for the apparent difference in sex interest.

School programs occasionally distracted from the day's work. In one week, for example, Friday was a holiday, and a beautiful early spring day as well, and although the children were paid and came willingly to the appointment, they were more or less excited and were evidently eager to get back to the playground.

The question of practice by the children between the experimental periods was approached with some misgiving. The writer, however, has no evidence that there was any significant amount of outside practice. Explanation was made on the first day that the work had nothing to do with school standing, that it was an experiment to see how boys and girls learned to do things they had never done before, and that it would spoil the experiment if a child practiced between times. The children were asked to be very careful not to try any of the tests except with the experimenter. The advisability of taking parents into confidence in the matter was considered and finally abandoned, because it was feared that attempted explanations would arouse rather than allay curiosity and result in interference. The nature of the series of tasks makes the' writer believe that children would not attempt to practice outside of school anyway. Arrangement for the mirror drawing would be some trouble to provide. To do the formboard and shorthand work would be almost out of the question. To practice the arithmetic, the child would have to compute the several multiplications in writing. The alphabet and drawing game might be somewhat easier to do, but would require getting materials together. The reproduction would be quite easy to go over, but after one or two repetitions it does not have any particular interest for the average child. In addition, the facts that each child had already spent an hour on the tasks each day, that most of them had only a limited amount of free indoor time on school days, that the tasks demanded a rather high degree of effort and concentration, that all the children readily agreed not to practice or to talk about them between experiments, and, finally, that nothing in the results suggests outside practice, lead the writer to believe that little, if any, outside work was done.

### THE LEARNING TASKS

Since standardized learning problem material for children nine and twelve years old is not available, endeavor was made to select a series of tasks differing in kind and appeal to children's interests, relatively novel to children, and requiring situations not strikingly artificial or restricted for their performance. The following were adopted:

1. Tracing the Starch star in a mirror, hereafter called the "Star" experiment.
2. Memorizing a multiplication table, $67 \times 2$, etc., hereafter called the "arithmetic" experiment.
3. Writing the alphabet with numbers— a 1  b 2  c 3 . . . z 26, hereafter called the "mixed series" experiment.
4. Placing the blocks in the Goddard Formboard with the eyes blindfolded, hereafter called the "Formboard" experiment.
5. Discovering the underlying principle in a game, hereafter called the "Drawing Game" experiment.
6. Learning to recognize shorthand characters, hereafter called the "Shorthand" experiment.
7. Reproducing orally a description read aloud by another, hereafter called the "Reproduction" experiment.

The experiments were performed individually by each subject on five days. In most of the cases these days were successive, from Monday to Friday, but in a few instances, due to absences or failure to find time for the work, a day was skipped and the final work was done on Saturday. In a very few cases it was necessary to go to the child's home to secure the last part of the series. It was impracticable to have each child work at the same hour or in the same place each day. In view of this fact an effort was made to avoid having to meet such a situation with the children. Criticism is fair at this point in that the results might have been different had all children done the work under the same conditions of time, surroundings, and the like. It does not follow, however, that, had such factors been constant, the differences between groups would have been other than they now appear. Table 4 gives the schedule of practice approximately followed in all cases. From about forty-five to seventy-five minutes was taken by each child each day. The capital letter "R" in the schedule is explained in the next section and means a retention test. A detailed description of the tests and their administration and scoring follow.

1. *Mirror Star Tracing.* The apparatus used was the mirror star tracing frame sold by Stoelting & Co. An adjustable shield intervenes between the eyes and the paper lying before the mirror, but the subject can see the reflection of the star in the glass by looking over the top of the shield into the mirror. Star outlines on mimeographed paper were used. These were securely fastened by thumb tacks to a small drawing board laid upon the stand of the apparatus. A short, soft-grade lead pencil was used, the point being somewhat dulled.

A brief explanation of the apparatus was given the subject and the purpose of the task was explained, emphasis being made upon keeping the pencil on the line and not lifting it up from the paper. When it seemed clear that the task was understood, the pencil was placed by the experimenter at the starting point and then grasped by the subject, who was directed to proceed. Later, when doing the experimental trials described in the next paragraph the subjects were directed to lower the shield,

TABLE 4
SCHEDULE OF DAILY PRACTICE AND TESTS

| | Day | | | | | Total |
|---|---|---|---|---|---|---|
| | 1 | 2 | 3 | 4 | 5 | |
| 1. Star ................ | 5′ | 5′ | 2 | 3 | 4 | 9 |
| 2. Arithmetic .......... | 1 | 2 | 2 | R 1 | R 1 | 7+2 |
| 3. Mixed Series ........ | 1 | 2 | 2 | 2 | 2 | 9 |
| 4. Formboard .......... | 1 | 2 | 3 | 3 | 3 | 12 |
| 5. Drawing Game ...... | 30 | 30 | 30 | 30 | 30 | 150 |
| 6. Shorthand .......... | 1 | 2 | 2 | R 1 | R 1 | 7+2 |
| 7. Reproduction ........ | 1 | 1 | 1 | R 1 | R 1 | 5+2 |
| 8. Star ................ | 5′ | 1 | 2 | 3 | 3 | 9 |

place the pencil at the starting point themselves, and then adjust the shield. This was done in part to save time, in part to make sure that the shield was properly placed, and in part to make the task a little more complete and interesting to the child.

Three five-minute practice periods were provided before the trials of the experiment proper were begun. As shown in the schedule, these practices took place the first and last thing on the first day, and the first thing on the second day. During these periods the children were cautioned and encouraged as far as it seemed necessary to secure their best effort to do as well as they could. With some of the younger children, especially the lower I.Q. subjects, considerable encouragement was needed to keep them at the task, as they wanted to give up after finding difficulty in controlling the pencil. It frequently was necessary also to caution others to keep the pencil on the paper. In all such directions care was taken to avoid suggestion to go slower, or in the opposite direction, or to be careful. Such suggestions as "Don't lift up the pencil," "Keep trying," "Make it go," "Try to keep on the line," "Get back on the line," etc., were used. The purpose of all such directions was to secure the best effort of the subject to make a good tracing.

The order of the experimental trials is shown in the schedule. Subjects soon discovered that time was kept for each trial, and to offset this emphasis, briefer or fuller attention was called to the merits of the tracings as they were completed. In only a few cases did it seem that the children were trying to make fast time regardless of quality of work. It is the belief of the writer that in most cases he was successful in keeping the idea of merit uppermost in the minds of the subjects.

On the last day, after completing the last trial, each subject made one tracing with direct vision, the paper being placed as before on the drawing board, which was put in its former position but not in the apparatus frame.

Time was taken with a stop-watch for each trial, and this record forms the basis of the score. Errors were also counted. No objective and reliable scheme was discovered for counting the errors on the stars as traced in this experiment. The Starch rule —every change in direction made off the line—was used as the basis for the count made. An original set of rules was added to this with the hope of making the count more nearly uniform and of penalizing tracings obviously inferior. After counting all the stars once, a recount was made with the use of a reading glass, which made it somewhat easier to detect changes in direction. The second count is the one used in this study. The fact that

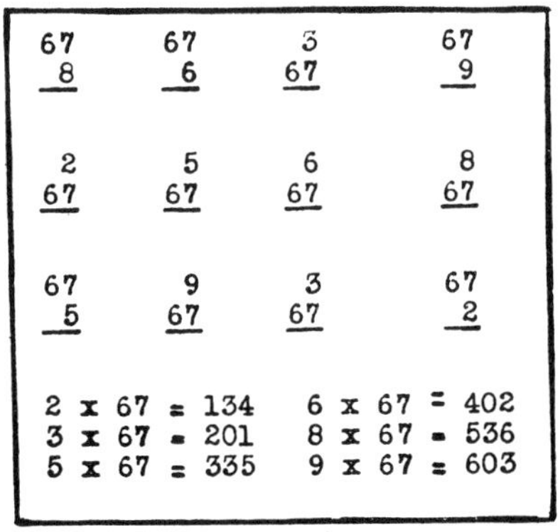

```
67      67      3       67
 8       6      67       9

 2       5       6       8
67      67      67      67

67       9       3       67
 5      67      67        2

2 x 67 = 134   6 x 67 = 402
3 x 67 = 201   8 x 67 = 536
5 x 67 = 335   9 x 67 = 603
```

Figure 1
Arithmetic Practice Card

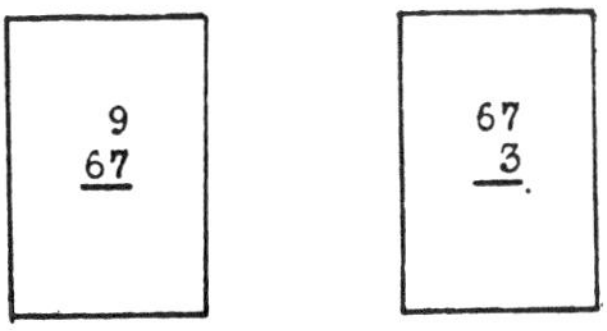

```
 9              67
67               3
```

Figure 1a
Arithmetic Test Cards

this second count was made after preliminary practice in counting errors on considerably over one thousand tracings, is given as sufficient grounds for its reliability, such as it may have, rather than the, at best, unsatisfactory list of rules aiming to define errors.

2. *Arithmetic.* Figure 1 shows the practice card used with each drill at the beginning of the experiment. Subjects were told that they were to learn some multiplication, were shown the card, and were directed to practice by saying each combination aloud, looking below, finding and saying the answer aloud. The method was illustrated with the first combination, the experimenter pointing to it and reading it aloud, showing the subject how to find the answer, and telling him to read it aloud. The child then proceeded with the next combination in the top row, being helped if necessary. In the case of some of the younger children, help was given in saying the numbers, "times," and "equals." The entire card was thus practiced. Then it was taken away, and small flash cards, each bearing a combination given on the practice card, were shown one by one, and the children were asked to give the answer if they could "remember" it. Older children were directed not to multiply in their heads but

to try to "just remember" the answer. Possibly with 67 × 2, 67 × 3, and 67 × 5 there may have been mental multiplication. Care was taken in the test to present first to the older children a combination in its reversed form, that is, with 67 as the multiplier, before the common form was shown. There was no time limit on the tests. In general, each child had all the time he wanted. In some cases answers were immediate; in others, children hung on to the card by verbalizing "a" or "m" etc., for many seconds. The purpose of the test was to find out which combinations every child had really memorized.

The method used for the second practice, on the second to the fifth days, was a little different from that of the first practices. Instead of having the subject go over the card in order, the experimenter pointed with a pencil to the combinations in random order, for the purpose of counteracting any possible tendency to memorize by location or by order. Flash cards were shuffled for each test, with the precaution added of going through them and separating any chance succession of the two forms of the same combination. On the third day, when the subjects had the work pretty well in hand, one other change was made to economize time, namely, the children were instructed to omit the oral reading of the combination and to recite aloud only each answer.

As the faster learning subjects mastered the practice card reproduced here, other similar cards, including additional combinations and their answers, were given them. This arrangement had its drawbacks but was deemed necessary, for the reason that the preliminary experiment seemed to show that some of the younger, dull children could not handle more than twelve combinations with any probability of scoring anything, while no children would probably get all twelve correct on the first practice. These conclusions proved to be correct. The question, then, of when to add combinations and how many to add at a time had to be determined. Arbitrarily the rule here given was followed: When a subject gives the correct answers to all but one of the combinations (this might mean two incorrect or omitted answers), add the next two combinations (four forms, two in the usual order, two in reversed order). The combinations 67 × 10 and 10 × 67 were not used. The most obvious drawback to such a scheme is that it reduces the learning of the added combinations to only those trials which follow introduction. It usually results in a decrease in the number of correct answers on the first test following the introduction of the combinations, the effect being, for the time, apparently an interference with learning already under way.

Record was made of the answers given by the subject. He was not informed which were right or which were wrong, but after the second test each day, he was told how many correct and how many wrong answers he had given.

When the arithmetic task was taken up on the fourth and fifth days, a test of retention over the intervening twenty-four hours was made before practice was given. This was done in exactly the same way as all other arithmetic tests were carried out, namely, by successively presenting the single flash cards to the subject and recording his responses. On these days, accordingly, there was but one practice.

3. *Mixed Series.* Younger children were asked if they knew the alphabet and, if doubt arose, they were asked to repeat it. In the case of one bright nine-year-old and two or three dull children it was not very well known. A very few oral practices were given before these children started the task. In a few instances children could not remember how to make certain letters. When it seemed clear they could not remember, they were shown how to make them. All such irregularity affects only the nine-year-old children, and of those, mainly the dull ones, whose results are, as would be expected in this task, far below those of the older children.

The instructions for this task were simple and readily grasped by every subject. "I want you to write the alphabet for me with little letters, like this (illustrating with small "a" script), and then to put a number after each letter." The experimenter wrote a 1, b 2, as he had directed the children, and then, after writing "c," he asked, "What number comes next?" In every case the child answered "3." He was then directed to begin and to "do it all the way through to z 26." Care was necessary to see that the order of letter, then number, was strictly followed, and that devices such as writing the numbers in the upper part of the space something like exponents were not used.

Time was taken for each trial with a stop-watch. Errors were also counted, everything irregular, omissions, duplications, writing over, being counted as errors.

4. *Goddard Formboard.* Subjects replaced the blocks in their proper places in the board with their eyes blindfolded.

Preceding the experimental trial of the first day all subjects were given two practices in replacing the blocks with eyes open. The directions were brief and to all appearances perfectly clear to all subjects. They were shown the board with the blocks in place; it was explained and illustrated, by two or three blocks, that each block had a place where it belonged; all blocks were then rapidly removed by the experimenter and placed in random order in a row of four piles along the farther side of the board. The subject was directed to "put them back where they belong, without making any mistakes." Time was taken for the trial and reported to the subject. The experimenter removed the blocks again, directing the child to keep his hands at his sides until told to start, and then instructed the subject to replace them again "faster this time." Time was again noted and reported to the subject. Then before further observation of the board could be made the experimenter blindfolded the subject. The blocks were then removed, and the subject was directed to replace them once more, being assured that he was to do "just the same thing." After each experimental trial the time was recorded and announced to the subject. All handling of the blocks between trials was done by the experimenter, and board and blocks were kept from the subject's view during the entire series for the remainder of the week.

No comments or suggestions were made by the experimenter during the trials, except when necessary to secure the continued effort of some of the children, who either thought they were through or gave up and did nothing, and in a very few cases when, after working many minutes without placing a piece, a subject was encouraged to continue by such a statement as, "There's a place for every piece," or "Keep trying." Errors were counted, each attempt to place a piece in a wrong recess being considered an error, provided the piece touched either the bottom or the inner edge of the recess; but continued efforts with the same piece at the same place were not counted as additional errors. If, however, an attempt was made to place a piece in a second recess and then effort was resumed at the first place, the resumed attempt was counted as an additional error. Subjects were not told that errors were being counted and no report on them was made to the children.

5. *Drawing Game.* This task is a modification of the somewhat familiar parlor game in which two players alternate drawing either one or two from a given number of pieces with the object of winning the last piece. Success requires the application of a principle: viz., that one's opponent must be forced to draw from a multiple of three; and a corollary, that when one's opponent draws from a multiple of three his draw must be so matched that on all succeeding draws he is forced to draw from a multiple of three. This is accomplished by matching a draw of one with a draw of two, or a draw of two with a draw of one. Certain uniform conditions were established for purposes of the experiment. Paper clips were used for the pieces. Each subject had thirty trials each day. A trial was considered to be the series of "draws involved in the reduction of any initial number of (clips) to 0, regardless of whether S (the subject) wins or losses." [3]  When the subject had won three times in succession with each number it was considered that he had "learned" that particular step. Draws were then made successively from 5, 7, 8, 10, 11, 13, 14, 16, and 17 clips, or as far as the subject worked in the 150 trials of the series. The subject drew first from each of these steps. Beginning with 5 clips, a check was made on the mastery of each step, as evidenced by his three successive wins, by having the experimenter draw first, but in such a way that the subject could win the trial if he drew correctly. These intervening trials also required that the subject win three successive times, and they are designated in the report as c5, c7, c8, etc. Under these conditions of first draws it was possible, then, for the subject to win every trial. In case of any error on his part, however, the experimenter so drew that the subject lost that trial.

The child was told that he would be shown how to play a game, but that he was to learn how to play it so that he would always win. The game was carefully explained and illustrated with three clips. It was made clear from the beginning and

[3] Peterson, J. C., *The Higher Mental Processes in Learning.* Psychological Monographs, Vol. XXVIII, No. 7, p. 3, 1920.

restated at numerous points during the series that if the subject drew correctly he would always win, but if he made a mistake he would lose. Before beginning the experimental trials with 4 clips the subject was given practice with 3, to insure that he understood the conditions of the drawings and recognized the outcome. Whether or not this knowledge remained with him when 4 clips were used at the beginning of the experiment cannot be proved. In a few cases, results seemed to indicate that it had momentarily been lost through the disconcerting effect, perhaps, of a different number of clips, but care was taken to emphasize the points in concrete form as trials proceeded. When the subject had won once with 4 clips, he was told that he must win three times in succession. Having accomplished that, 5 clips were used. Then, when he had "learned" that difficulty, he was told to see if he could win when the experimenter drew first, that if he drew right he would always win.

Beginning with the step of 7 clips, those subjects who had not already discovered the fact were asked, when 3 clips were left, if they could tell who would win. This soon established the significance of 3. Thereafter, when subjects voluntarily stopped drawing with 3 clips remaining, the rest of the draws for that trial were omitted. When any subject continued to draw from 3, he was permitted to do so until he voluntarily discontinued making this last draw.

Beginning with step 8 and continuing through c10 the question, "Can you tell who's going to win?" was put to the subject whenever he so drew as to force the experimenter to draw from 6. This was done to aid the children indirectly to see the significance of that multiple of 3. Preliminary trial had demonstrated that too much help would be given by carrying this directing of attention to 3 and 6 on to 9. Without such suggestion with the 3 and the 6, the task seemed to be too hard for even the bright twelve-year-old children used in preliminary work. The writer does not claim, however, that the preliminary work did more than suggest what might be the necessary indirect help in developing the concept of the significance of these numbers.

A certain regularity in the experimenter's draws was necessary. It was found that the subject might win by remembering a lucky sequence of draws when playing with the smaller numbers. To offset this possibility, the experimenter changed his first draw whenever the subject made a win. The experimenter made other changes in his "after-the-first-draw" with numbers 10 and above for the purpose of further insuring that subjects were not working on memorization alone. While this latter precaution was really not necessary, as the change in the experimenter's first draw would upset the success of mere memorized

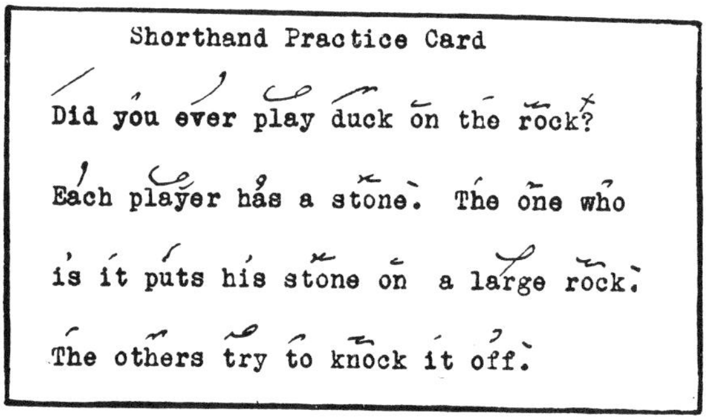

Figure 2
Shorthand Practice Card

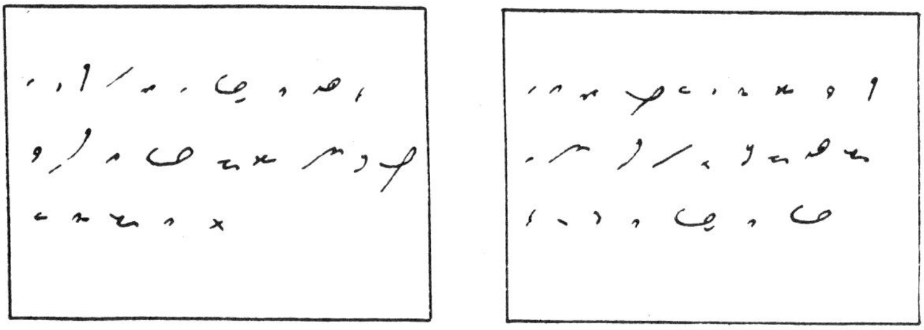

Figure 2a
Shorthand Test Cards

sequences, it was carried out for all subjects who worked with 10 or more clips.

When a subject had worked through c10 and if he showed evidences of working on some principle, he was asked to tell how he determined his draws. Such a question as "How should you draw so you can always win?" or "What's the trick in the game?" usually secured an effort to formulate a rule, but the language difficulty of putting ideas into words was very great. For that reason no use is made of these answers in this study. The procedure is reported because it was followed.

Record was made of all draws and of the cumulative number of trials required to master each difficulty. The latter forms the basis for the measures used in the report.

6. *Shorthand.* Figures 2 and 2a show the practice and test cards for this task.

The procedure in this task was similar to that in the arithmetic task, except that the experimenter guided the response of the subjects in all practice work by deliberately pointing to each character with a pencil. It was explained to the subject that the marks stood for the words underneath, and that he was to learn the marks. Then he was directed to look at the mark as the experimenter pointed to it and to say aloud the word for which it stood. On the first trial on the first three days, the passage was read in direct order. On the other practices the experimenter pointed to characters in random order. Every character was thus directly connected with the printed word for which it stood, once in each practice. A test was made after each practice by presenting the subject with a card upon which appeared the characters alone, arranged in different order from that of the practice card. The subject was asked to translate the characters. Two such test cards were used, care being taken to alternate them.

The record was the number of correct recognitions indicated by the subject. As in the arithmetic tests, the subject was not informed which recognitions were correct, but after the second test each day he was told how many rights and how many wrongs he had scored. As was the case in the arithmetic series, two retention tests were given, one the first thing when the shorthand task was reached on days four and five.

7. *Reproduction.* The following description, which is an adaptation and extension of Test 11 of the Herring Revision of the Binet-Simon Tests, was used. The lines crossing the print indicate the division into ideas as counted in the tests, a total of 48.

The subject was directed to listen carefully to a "story" so that he could retell it. The experimenter read the selection aloud, distinctly and with little emphasis or expressive interpretation. At the conclusion the subject was directed to tell everything he could remember. There was no time limit, each subject being allowed as much time as he apparently could use to any purpose. In case very little was reproduced encouragement was given by such direction as "Go ahead," "What else?" etc. In a few cases where the results were particularly meager urging was

In a little | cottage | on the banks | of a river | in France | there lived a farmer | and his wife. | Their home was | in a pleasant spot; | behind it | was a forest; | in front | was a maple | tree. | Under its branches | there sat their daughter | a good | and gentle girl, | whose work it was | to look after the sheep | of her father's | flock. | The name of Goldie | might have been given her | as | her hair was golden | brown, | while | her red | cheeks, | smiling | dark | eyes | and bright | lips | gave one delight | to behold. | But | she was called Gloria | by her father, | Sunshine | by those who knew her | well, | and Fairy | Girl | by her mother's | little | sister. |

FIGURE 3.   Reproduction.

continued, but nearly always with not a single added idea. Apparently after a minute or so nothing further came to mind, either for the fast or for most of the slow reproducers.

The record was the number of ideas correctly given, identical wording not being required. When words of the selection were incorrectly used, however, they were not counted, as, for instance: "her father called her Goldie" (not correct). "Goldie," the word incorrectly used, was not counted. On the other hand, when single words, such as "river," "cottage," and the like, were given—as happened with a few of the younger dull subjects—they were counted if they were important words in any idea group. This concession affected the scores of but the dull nine-year-olds and can only slightly have reduced the differences between them and the other groups, differences which, with the procedure followed, are very striking. When this task was reached on the fourth and fifth days, a retention test was given before the selection was read aloud.

# CHAPTER III

## THE MEASURES USED AND THE TREATMENT OF THE DATA

### The Measures

For the star, the mixed series, and the formboard tasks, the time consumed for each trial was converted into rate of work per 1,000 seconds, the multiplication of the reciprocals being for the purpose of removing decimal places. This converted score has two advantages: it gives rising curves as the other task results furnish, and it puts the measures into units of amount of work accomplished, similar to those for arithmetic, shorthand, and reproduction, though computed on a different basis. To secure these rate figures from the time measures, the original time for each trial of each subject was changed into its reciprocal, carried out to five decimal places.

For the arithmetic, shorthand, and reproduction tasks the amount of correct work done was the measure. The unit for this measure was one practice. Time was controlled relatively, that is, each subject, working continuously on the task, worked at his own "normal" rate. Care was exercised that he did not pause during practice for the apparent purpose of mentally going over any part of the work. This would have been most easily done in the unguided arithmetic practices. In only a few cases was there any tendency to do so, and in such cases the subjects were immediately directed to continue with the oral practice. Subjects seemed to be set almost from the start to carry practices along without delay or variation in method. After the first few trials this was especially marked. Unintentional interferences seemed to act as annoyances. The writer does not believe that recall or special emphasis on any parts of the tasks during a practice occurred to any appreciable extent.

In the guided arithmetic and the shorthand practice, the experimenter endeavored to control the time so that each subject would work at a comfortable but continuous rate. The pencil, as pointer, was held at each item for about one second after the oral response had been given by the subject and was then moved to another item to which the subject at once reacted in his own normal time. The description for reproduction was read at as nearly a uniform rate as the experimenter was able to follow, about 55 seconds for each reading. Metronome, buzzer, or other artificial contrivance for indicating time was purposely avoided in the belief that such would have added unreality to the situation, and would have interfered with the normal reaction of subjects in normal learning situations.

The difference in the maturity of the subjects is further reason for making amount of practice rather than amount of time the constant in the arithmetic and shorthand tasks. The difficulty of saying the numbers and reading the words for the shorthand characters was such, in the case of many of the nine-year-old children, that had the time necessary for them to go once through the material been the fixed amount of time for all, the brighter children would, no doubt, have gone over the cards many times at each practice. Conversely, had the time required by the bright twelve-year-old children for going once through the material been the fixed amount of time for all, many of the nine-year-old children would have gone over but a small portion of the practice cards. It was not the purpose of the study to measure differences under such conditions—which obviously would have been very great—but rather to investigate, if possible, differences when all subjects had an equal amount of practice. The thesis is proposed that many practices by one individual on a given task, in a certain length of time, are no more equal to, or identical with one practice by another individual in the same length of time, than is one practice by the former individual in a given number of minutes equal to, or identical with one practice by the latter individual in fewer or more minutes. It is under the condition of equal amount of practice that the products are compared in the arithmetic, shorthand, and reproduction tasks.

In the drawing game, the same general conditions were considered the basis of practice, except that no direct effort at all was made to control the time of responses. Each subject was allowed to take his own time. Total time spent on this task each day was noted, however, and the averages of the total time in minutes for the 150 trials for the four groups are as given in the following tabulation:

| Group ........ | D 9 | Br 9 | D 12 | Br 12 |
|---|---|---|---|---|
| Minutes ...... | 44 | 42 | 39 | 43 |

The differences are not significant, apparently.  The question of the task is: Given all the time they wish, how do subjects compare in their ability to progress through a series of similar problems of varying difficulty?

Several factors enter into measuring achievement in this task. Obviously the first number used—4—is not as difficult as most of the higher numbers.  The same is true in lesser degree of 5, 7, and 8.  Difficulty, however, does not increase by equal amounts, in any probability, and, as subjects begin to form the concept of the principle underlying successful drawings, the difficulty decreases until there is none left but that of keeping some simple arithmetic straight.

Number correct is not a satisfactory measure of learning, as, under the conditions of the experiment, a subject might alternate wins and losses on, say, the step for 7—as was actually the case —and thereby collect a fairly high percentage of wins without getting very far in learning the principle, while another might go directly through the 7's, collecting but six wins on that step, work through 8 and 10 with many losses and few wins, and at the end of the series be nearer a mastery of the task than the former subject, but have considerably fewer wins to his credit.

After much statistical experimentation, it was decided to use the average cumulative number of trials per difficulty of the best two-thirds of each group as far as they learned the game.  While this reduces the number of cases to ten or eleven per group, it in a sense includes them all, because it selects the same parts of four assumed normal distributions, each of which is made up of all the cases in the several groups.  Averages of all fifteen records of each group would be very false data in that some individuals might contribute, say, 100 trials to one difficulty and nothing to the next.  The measure used shows results very much like those which the percentages of subjects of each group learning each difficulty—a truer measure of the entire group—reveal, and has the advantage of giving averages, the terms of the measures used in the other tasks.

## THE RECORDS

1. Real averages of actual scores were computed[1] for each group in each task and, in addition, the average number of errors in the star experiment. Learning curves for these averages are shown. Averages rather than medians were used with even this small number of cases because, since they contain all the scores, they are more representative of the data than are medians.

2. Reliability indices with the small number of cases of this study are not very significant. They are given in terms of medians and Q's, first, because medians and Q's are easier to compute than averages and sigmas; and second, because medians are more appropriate in some cases where the distributions are not very close to the normal curve.

Reliability of the median is based on the formula:

$$P.E._{\text{median}} = \frac{5}{4} \cdot \frac{Q}{\sqrt{N}}$$

Reliability of the difference is based on the formula:

$$P.E._{\text{diff. mdn. 1 mdn. 2}} = \sqrt{P.E.^2_{\text{mdn. 1}} + P.E.^2_{\text{mdn. 2}}}$$

Reliability of Q is based on the formula:

$$\sigma_Q = \frac{1.65\, Q}{\sqrt{2N}}$$

3. Psychographs and overlapping of groups are presented in terms of total scores made in each task and on the basis of the medians and Q's of the entire sixty cases as one group, individual deviation from those medians being converted into terms of Q's for the whole group.

4. In Chapter VI, where minor points are treated, the derivation and treatment of the records there presented are explained.

[1] See footnote on page 21 of Chapter IV.

# CHAPTER IV

## RESULTS: GROUP ACCOMPLISHMENT

### FINDINGS

From the averages for the various tasks and groups,[1] graphs of learning curves have been drawn and are indicated in Figs. 4 to 11. The bulk of the discussion of results is based on these curves.

Study of learning curves is difficult because the value of units is not known, because the zero point is not located, and because the nature, extent, and relationships of functions involved in any one product or in all are not known. In the data of this report, however, certain factors are, within limits, defined and controlled—ages of the subjects, intelligence as measured by a supposedly reliable test, and the stimulation situations to which the subjects responded—and certain striking resemblances and differences are revealed by the curves. These will be indicated for all the graphs and then briefly discussed.

The graphs fall into four quite distinct types.

*Type I—Arithmetic and Shorthand.* Beginning with Test 3, the differences of the medians are much better than chance between all groups,[2] and final differences between D 9 and Br 9, D 12 and Br 12, and D 12 and Br 9 range from about 95 chances in 100 to practical certainty. The general order on all tests, from low to high scores, is D 9, D 12, Br 9, and Br 12. At the beginning of the arithmetic series D 12 and Br 9 are practically together, but they soon diverge, certainly from Test 3 on, and their divergence is the most pronounced of all. The same general facts are true for the shorthand. Br 9 and Br 12 do not seem to tend to separate or to come together as far as gross differences are concerned. The rise of the curves does not seem to

---

[1] These tables of averages have been omitted in the publication of this study; they are on file in the office of the registrar of Teachers College, Columbia University, and may be found there.
[2] *Ibid.*

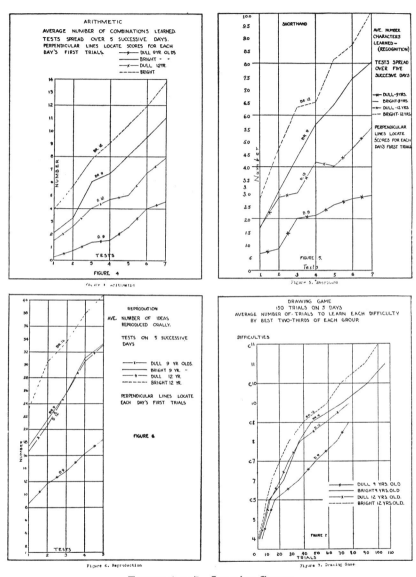

FIGURES 4 TO 7. Learning Curves.

indicate approaching plateaus or physiological limits, unless possibly with the dull groups. The conditions of the experiment, however, may be the cause of this slope, as the retention tests, scores of which do not appear in the curves, were given before Tests 6 and 7, and the practice from these tests may have raised the scores of Tests 6 and 7. The general trend of the four curves, their relative positions, and the regularity of their rise are clear and unmistakable.

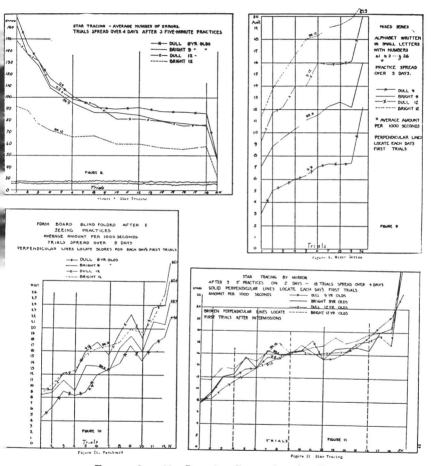

FIGURES 8 TO 11. Learning Curves (*continued*)

*Type II—Reproduction, Drawing Game, and Star Errors.* The table [3] of the differences of the medians between D 9 and Br 9 and between D 12 and Br 12 shows that there are far better

[3] See footnote on page 21.

than chance differences at all difficulties in the reproduction and drawing game. Because of the unreliability of the star error count, its statistical reliability is not given. In all three tasks the general order from low to high scores is clearly D 9, Br 9 and D 12 together, and Br 12. The closeness of the curves for D 12 and Br 9—groups of almost identical average mental ages— is striking. Significance is added to this relationship by the frequency with which the individuals of these groups keep together; this is shown in the psychographs in Chapter V. There is no apparent tendency for the reproduction curves to converge or diverge in relation to one another, unless possibly D 9 rises less rapidly than the others. The rise of these curves may be affected, as in the case of arithmetic and shorthand, by retention tests given before Tests 4 and 5. In the drawing game graph it seems that, although D 12 and Br 9 keep relatively near together at first, the Br 9 tend to draw away from the others in the direction of the Br 12 when the more difficult steps are reached. The slope of these curves indicates the unevenness of the difficulties of the different steps. The rapid early rise through difficulties 4 and 5 is followed by a decline in slope that continues throughout the steps considered in the graph. The progress of the few bright subjects who solved the problem, and also that of others who came nearer the solution than the averages, show that soon after difficulty c11 the task becomes easier and the curves rise again rapidly.

The curve for star errors is included in this group because it evidently belongs here. Strictly speaking, error measures should not be compared with amount of work measures, but in this task the thing that the error count is attempting to measure—quality of work—is measured by work actually done, but incorrectly done. When the subject does work off the line, it is counted as one or more errors. Thus in a real sense the star errors are measures of amount of work. As the amount of work incorrectly done in this task decreases, errors decrease, and consequently the error curves fall as improvement takes place.

The unreliable nature of the count of errors requires tentative interpretation of the curves. If the early tracings of the dull 9 group (D 9) had been more severely penalized than they were, as probably should have been done, the first part of that curve would have been higher on the chart, and the graph would then have been strikingly like that of the reproduction curves in the relationship shown between groups. Possibly later discussion will lead to the belief that it would be expected to show such a likeness.

With the exception of the first part of the curve for D 9, there is no clear change in the relative positions of the curves among the four groups. The lines fall somewhat more rapidly at first. When it is considered that the data for these curves come from work done after fifteen minutes of practice not presented here, it may rather safely be assumed that, had the errors for the entire work on the star been measured, the decline at the beginnings of the curves would have been very steep. Apparently all groups had improved greatly and had reached the stage where their rate of improvement was decreasing markedly at the time the records begin. The points beyond the end of the curves on the ordinate marked "D. V.," Fig. 8, show how far the subjects were from possible accomplishment. The gradual decline in their curves from about trial 8 suggests how slowly they would probably approach direct vision ability. There is nothing to indicate which group would first have reached these points if practice had been continued indefinitely.

The three graphs of this group show a striking similarity in the relationships between groups, and, for each curve separately, an unmistakable evenness and regularity in slope and a general trend that is clear.

*Type III—Mixed Series and Formboard.* The table [4] of differences of the medians shows that in the mixed series all differences are far better than chance. In part because of the great amount of variability and irregularity of improvement in the formboard, differences in this task are only little better than mere chance statistical differences. Very clearly for the former and, although confused by variations of chance factors, apparently for the latter, the order from low to high is D 9, Br 9, D 12, and Br 12. This order is distinctly different from that of Types I and II.

In the mixed series, the gross differences between all groups seem to increase, resulting in a fan-like divergence of the curves. In the formboard they do so somewhat. There may be a tend-

[4] See footnote on page 21.

ency in the formboard test for the bright 9 to draw toward the
dull 12 and away from the dull 9.  The cases are too few and
the test series is too short to justify more than raising the question.

In the mixed series curves, flattening appears for all groups,
but more markedly for the dull—although they do not come, in
gross differences, as near to normal performance when the letters
and numbers are written separately as do the bright groups.
In the formboard curves, very little, if any, tendency to flattening seems to be present.

While the curves for the formboard fail to show as clear relationships or as even and regular slopes as do those for the mixed
series, there do seem to be unmistakable tendencies of the same
character in them, and therefore the two graphs are grouped
together.  It may be that the formboard belongs somewhere between the mixed series and the star time, next considered.

*Type IV—Star Time.*  This graph seems to fit in with none
of the other types.  The differences,[5] except at the beginning,
are no better than chance, although a tendency for the bright
to be high and the dull to be low may be present, especially at
first.  The striking facts are the certainty of improvement for
all groups, the closeness of their successive scores from trial 4
on, and the erratic crossing and recrossing of their curves.
Chance factors no doubt greatly disturb the evenness of learning
in this task, and the variability is very great.

## Discussion

Five points will be considered in the following discussion.

1. *Selection of the Subjects.*  Because of the small number in
each group, it may be that one or more of the groups were made
up of children particularly competent in one or another respect.
Such selected groups would therefore show to advantage in certain tasks.  While it is conceded that with this small number
of cases the selection may not be a true sampling, two objections
can be made to such an explanation for the results which appear.
First, the selection of subjects from three different schools and
two different school systems would make the probability of such

' See footnote on page 21.

special selection remote. Second, there is no indication in the results of the experiment as a whole that any one group had any outstanding advantage of this sort. Suppose, for example, that the bright nine-year-old group were of ability above the average for all bright nine-year-old children in learning arithmetic. Why should that group score also above the D 12 group in shorthand, but only the same as D 12 in reproduction, the drawing game, and star errors, below D 12 in the mixed series and formboard, and just about like all the groups in star time? A more plausible explanation is that the group did very well in arithmetic and shorthand, moderately well in reproduction, drawing game, and star errors, and not so well in mixed series and formboard because the tasks demanded abilities possessed in varying degrees by the different groups by reason of the selective factors, age and brightness, operating to determine the groups. Further, the amounts of the differences in arithmetic, shorthand, reproduction, drawing game, star errors, mixed series, and in some respects in the formboard, are so great and so variously related for the groups that it seems altogether improbable that undetected, special, selective factors, other than those upon which the selection was made, would account for the differences. Study of the curves gives no indication that the differences in accomplishment could be due to selection of individuals in one or another of the groups who were especially competent in any particular task.

2. *Conditions of the Experiment.* Use of amount of practice rather than time of practice as the basis to measure product might have resulted in such variation in time spent as to account for differences. The only tasks where this difference in time was considerable are the arithmetic and the drawing game tasks. In the shorthand and the reproduction tasks, time, as well as amount of practice, was practically constant. All the other tasks were timed. Differences between groups in the arithmetic, shorthand, reproduction, and drawing game apparently do not show any significant relation to amount of time used. As a matter of fact, in the arithmetic work the dull nine-year-old children spent a much longer time than the other groups in going over the practice card—largely because of their difficulty in saying the words and reading the numbers orally—and the bright twelve-year-olds were much more rapid in their practice than the other groups.

If time had been made equal, the differences would have been much greater than the records show.

In the case of star errors and the drawing game the records are not very satisfactory, in that, for the former, the record is a purely subjective determination, and for the latter the number of cases is reduced from 15 to 11 or 10. In other respects, there seems to be no reason to suppose the measures of the groups in any way failed to represent their relative abilities, unless the inability to determine the value of the units, the location of the zero points, and the nature, extent, and relationships of the functions involved invalidate the whole study.

3. *Differences Due to Chronological Age.* With the groups studied, difference in chronological age seems to accompany a difference in scores by children of the same I.Q., except, perhaps, in star time. In all other tasks, older children of the same I.Q. score better than the younger. But in arithmetic and shorthand the three years' difference does not mean as much as a difference of the 30 points in I.Q., while it practically does equalize that difference in reproduction, the drawing game, and star errors. In .the mixed series and the formboard the three years more than compensate for the 30 I.Q. points. Apparently age in years has value in varying degree, depending upon the task attempted.

4. *Differences Due to I.Q.* With the groups studied, the average difference of 30 I.Q. points more than compensates for the three years' difference in the arithmetic and shorthand. In reproduction, the drawing game, and star errors it seems to equalize that age difference, while in the formboard and mixed series it does not compensate for it for the period of practice covered by the experiment. Apparently I.Q. has value in varying degree, depending upon the task attempted.

5. *Differences in Responses.* Points 3 and 4, just made, lead directly to the supposition that differences appear because of the differences in the character of the responses required to meet the situations of the tasks. This matter will be considered, first, by indicating what selection of subjects the tasks make, and second, by an attempted analysis of the most obvious differences in the responses required by the tasks.

Type I—Arithmetic and Shorthand—distinguishes between bright and dull children of the life ages tested, and between bright and dull children of the same average mental age—about 10–5—when the life age difference is as much as 3 years. It also distinguishes children three years older from younger ones of the same brightness. In other words, the task calls for responses which those of the type of intelligence indicated by a relatively high I.Q. score can best give. Turning to the task it will be noted that this work called for motor responses mainly confined to the reading and speaking machinery of the subject, and mental responses of memorization of material in large part new to the subject. Compared with such a response as learning to swim or to ride a bicycle, this task might be considered as characterized by very little gross muscular movement. The motor responses required do not seem to be those in which older or brighter children can notably surpass younger or duller children, down to limits far below those existing in this study. The significant factors in the response seem to be of some other nature.

Type II—Reproduction, Drawing Game, and Star Errors—calls for responses such that those of mental age about 10–5 and chronological ages about 9 and 12 accomplish practically the same results notwithstanding a difference of 3 life years and 30 I.Q. points. It distinguishes subjects of different mental ages, however, giving those of the higher mental age the greater scores. In other words, these tasks call for responses which subjects of the same mental age can make about equally well, regardless of life age and physical maturity.

The reproduction task requires motor responses confined mainly to the hearing and speaking machinery of the subjects and the mental responses of holding in mind and expression of material in general familiar to the subjects. Thus, while this task might also be considered as characterized by very little gross muscular movement, yet it does not involve the difficulties present in the tasks of Type I in that the material (everyday ideas) is more familiar.

The drawing task requires motor responses, mainly confined to seeing and to moving clips with the hand, and for a considerable number of mental operations difficult to determine. Of these a few will probably be agreed upon: remembering the rules of the game, and the parts of previous draws, counting, and some sort of imagining, both recall and anticipatory. The first steps involve situations which might easily have been within the perceptual grasp of all subjects as signified by their spans of attention. Later difficulties make that possible only by draws which reduce the number of clips to 6, 5, or 4. To reduce to a number from which the subjects could visually see the end or result, required either remembering a lucky combination of draws or planful trial and error, with resulting formulation of conclusions. The slowness with which these conclusions came is indicated in the comparative decrease in slope of the curves beyond step c5. This task, then, also seems to be characterized by very little gross muscular movement, the first part of it involving difficulties quite possible of solution by perceptual trial and error learning. In so far as that is true, the task might then be like the reproduction task, since it requires mental responses of a familiar sort. The later difficulties would be more like those of arithmetic and shorthand, involving unfamiliar material such as drawing conclusions, and trial and error of a less practiced sort.

The star tracing requires motor responses of holding the pencil, making a mark with it, moving the hand along in the direction of the various sides of the star and, in regard to errors, inhibiting incorrect movements and building up new units of movements. This task is, then, one apparently largely motor, but, from the angle of quality, requiring inhibitions and integrations, qualities which involve finer motor control rather than gross muscular movement.

Type III—Mixed Series and Formboard—distinguishes most sharply between the chronological ages and selects the brighter from the dull when as many as 30 I.Q. points difference is present. In other words, the task calls for responses which children of older age can best give.

The mixed series requires motor responses of the writing mechanisms of the subjects and mental responses of recalling two known series, substituting one for the other at each successive step. Observation clearly indicated the very real motor difficulty of writing on the part of many of the younger subjects. The mental responses involved in integrating the two series may account for most of the differences between bright and dull of the same life ages.

In the formboard the task requires motor responses of handling blocks, finding the places for them and placing them therein, and mental responses of recognizing forms and spaces and remembering them in relation one to another. Apparently the older children can give these responses better than younger children, while the brighter ones of the same age do somewhat better than the dull. Both gross muscular movement and mental responses seem to be significant in these tasks.

Type IV—Star Time—calls for responses such that the three years of age and the 30 I.Q. points make scarcely any difference after a few practices. The responses involved have been indicated under Type II, star errors. Apparently, as far as getting over an amount of work of this nature is concerned, when quality of response is not distinguished, the demand is for a relatively gross muscular response, not significantly dependent upon control of a high quality of intellect as indicated by I.Q's, nor upon physical maturity as indicated by life age.

### CONCLUSIONS

Maturity as determined by life age or mental age, and brightness as determined by Binet I.Q., seem so to equip ordinary school children that, in proportion as tasks require less gross muscular movement, they will distinguish the mature from the less mature and the bright from the less bright.

# CHAPTER V

## RESULTS: INDIVIDUAL ACCOMPLISHMENT

### VARIABILITY

Variability of individuals from central tendencies of the groups is studied in three ways: first, by comparison of groups by means of the statistical measure, the coefficient of variability; second, by comparison of the frequency distributions of individual total scores; and third, by study of psychographs showing individual total scores for all tests or trials in each task.

### COEFFICIENT OF VARIABILITY

The formula used for computing the coefficient of variability is

$$\text{C.V.} = \frac{100 \times Q}{\text{Median}}$$

Table 5 gives the coefficients by groups and tasks.

In studying relative variability of groups by the several tasks, or that of tasks by the several groups, the influence of chance factors due to the few scores forming the distributions must be kept in mind. The unknown locations of zero points also bear upon the comparisons that appear. These two factors should, therefore, qualify any conclusions drawn from the table of coefficients of variability. Two or three tendencies are apparent, however, from the somewhat erratic variations shown in the table. First, if the figures for the four groups of subjects are compared task by task, it appears that the tasks tend to fall into the same types as were shown in Chapter IV. In arithmetic and shorthand, the dull 9 has the greatest amount of variation, dull 12 next, bright 9 third, and bright 12 fourth. In reproduction and the drawing game, dull 9 has the greatest amount of variation, bright 9 and dull 12 have about the same amount, and bright 12 has the least. In the mixed series and formboard, relations are not so clear, but it seems, on the whole, that dull 9

TABLE 5

COEFFICIENTS OF VARIABILITY COMPUTED FROM MEDIANS

|  | D 9 | Br 9 | D 12 | Br 12 |  |  | D 9 | Br 9 | D 12 | Br 12 |
|---|---|---|---|---|---|---|---|---|---|---|
| *Tests* |  | *Arithmetic* |  |  |  |  |  | *Shorthand* |  |  |
| 1 | 48.2 | 79.5 | 66.4 | 36.4 |  |  | 45.8 | 50.0 | 50.0 | 41.2 |
| 2 | 47.6 | 57.8 | 64.7 | 35.2 |  |  | 50.0 | 33.3 | 32.2 | 17.3 |
| 3 | 83.3 | 50.0 | 47.7 | 24.8 |  |  | 70.5 | 27.8 | 39.5 | 25.0 |
| 4 | 69.4 | 38.8 | 47.8 | 21.4 |  |  | 70.5 | 24.2 | 26.0 | 22.6 |
| 5 | 71.0 | 34.4 | 37.0 | 34.2 |  |  | 55.8 | 35.7 | 39.2 | 25.6 |
| 6 | 62.7 | 24.1 | 41.5 | 20.2 |  |  | 80.4 | 30.8 | 25.8 | 45.0 |
| 7 | 66.6 | 22.0 | 31.8 | 20.1 |  |  | 80.4 | 23.2 | 37.1 | 43.3 |
|  |  | *Reproduction* |  |  | *Diff'y* * |  |  | *Drawing Game* |  |  |
| 1 | 29.0 | 20.0 | 22.3 | 13.2 | 4 | 39.6 | 25.0 | 27.5 | 12.9 |
| 2 | 28.0 | 25.4 | 26.8 | 16.8 | 5 | 17.5 | 21.2 | 12.5 | 10.8 |
| 3 | 25.7 | 18.3 | 15.8 | 13.7 | c5 | 19.6 | 15.0 | 15.8 | 10.4 |
| 4 | 45.6 | 16.9 | 9.5 | 8.2 | 7 | 38.0 | 23.5 | 20.0 | 17.4 |
| 5 | 34.4 | 20.9 | 16.4 | 6.4 | c7 | 44.2 | 19.1 | 12.2 | 22.6 |
|  |  |  |  |  | 8 | 35.7 | 26.8 | 22.7 | 18.5 |
|  |  |  |  |  | c8 | 35.7 | 15.8 | 13.1 | 18.3 |
|  |  |  |  |  | 10 |  | 19.7 | 34.0 | 19.4 |
|  |  |  |  |  | c10 |  | 13.0 |  | 29.0 |
|  |  |  |  |  | 11 |  | 12.9 |  | 38.0 |
|  |  |  |  |  | c11 |  |  |  | 30.2 |
| *Trials* |  | *Mixed Series* |  |  |  |  | *Formboard* |  |  |  |
| 1 | 22.7 | 17.2 | 30.6 | 22.9 |  | 59.1 | 38.3 | 66.2 | 36.9 |
| 2 | 16.0 | 10.2 | 38.8 | 22.8 |  | 52.6 | 40.8 | 33.7 | 26.9 |
| 3 | 17.3 | 13.4 | 28.1 | 18.4 |  | 41.2 | 45.4 | 42.1 | 40.3 |
| 4 | 23.3 | 19.9 | 21.2 | 16.3 |  | 34.6 | 40.2 | 42.7 | 45.3 |
| 5 | 27.8 | 7.3 | 17.9 | 15.1 |  | 57.3 | 60.9 | 34.9 | 27.7 |
| 6 | 28.6 | 15.1 | 20.0 | 22.1 |  | 60.0 | 45.1 | 33.9 | 28.9 |
| 7 | 29.7 | 17.9 | 20.2 | 15.5 |  | 31.4 | 32.6 | 25.3 | 22.2 |
| 8 | 23.3 | 11.4 | 20.9 | 14.7 |  | 37.5 | 28.1 | 26.6 | 21.8 |
| 9 | 30.8 | 12.1 | 23.4 | 16.7 |  | 36.9 | 25.6 | 34.1 | 27.6 |
| 10 |  |  |  |  |  | 43.7 | 35.1 | 38.2 | 20.9 |
| 11 |  |  |  |  |  | 29.3 | 27.4 | 44.1 | 13.8 |
| 12 |  |  |  |  |  | 44.5 | 26.0 | 34.8 | 14.4 |
|  |  |  |  | *Star Time* |  |  |  |  |  |  |
| 1 | 31.2 | 41.9 | 32.9 | 43.2 | 10 | 18.0 | 9.3 | 20.8 | 21.4 |
| 2 | 27.1 | 50.0 | 29.9 | 33.4 | 11 | 17.1 | 15.2 | 17.2 | 14.4 |
| 3 | 55.7 | 40.0 | 23.2 | 22.8 | 12 | 15.7 | 16.8 | 13.0 | 19.7 |
| 4 | 21.2 | 32.3 | 14.4 | 27.9 | 13 | 23.2 | 29.9 | 8.6 | 22.9 |
| 5 | 29.6 | 17.8 | 16.6 | 31.5 | 14 | 23.5 | 22.3 | 18.8 | 19.2 |
| 6 | 27.3 | 23.2 | 16.2 | 27.4 | 15 | 26.1 | 20.4 | 18.0 | 22.4 |
| 7 | 19.0 | 25.3 | 9.8 | 15.6 | 16 | 21.3 | 11.4 | 21.6 | 20.0 |
| 8 | 21.4 | 12.0 | 11.7 | 20.0 | 17 | 11.8 | 18.2 | 22.4 | 21.9 |
| 9 | 12.9 | 13.5 | 16.0 | 18.5 | 18 | 10.5 | 13.8 | 10.7 | 32.3 |

* Diff'y stands for difficulty.

has the greatest amount of variations in the mixed series, dull 12 next, bright 12 third, and, for some reason not clear, bright 9 the least; while in the formboard, dull 9 has the greatest, dull 12 and bright 9 about the same, and bright 12 the least. In the star time differences are not at all apparent. All seem to vary unsteadily within much the same limits.

A second tendency appears in arithmetic, shorthand, and reproduction, in which dull 9 increases in variability as practice continues, while the other three groups decrease. The nature of the tasks may account for this. In each of these tasks the amount of material practiced was limited, because it was believed necessary to take that amount of material which would secure scores from the slowest children but would not secure maximum scores from the fastest children. Apparently the amount of material taken in these tasks was such that the best in the dull 9 group were not cut down very much on their possible scores throughout their entire practice, with the result that, as practice continued, they added just about all they would have added had there been more material. On the other hand, the best subjects in the other groups would probably have increased their scores had there been more material. Specifically, practice in arithmetic was begun with twelve forms of 6 combinations and continued with the same twelve until the subjects had learned all but one combination. Then four other forms (two new combinations) were added. If, instead of this the bright 9 and the twelve-year-old subjects had practiced at each succeeding trial, say, twice as many combinations as they had learned, or a number much in excess of their preceding scores, they would probably have scored higher than the tests, as administered, recorded for them. All the dull 9 subjects, however, best as well as poorest, learning so few of the twelve combinations, would probably have added very few correct answers above what the tests recorded even if there had been more material. Hence the variation between the best and the poorest was more nearly unhampered in this group than it was for the other groups.

In the shorthand, twenty-seven characters were practiced. For the dull 9 group this number, which seems to have been about all any of them could handle, was a sufficient number to indicate throughout the series the relatively true differences between best and poorest of the group. For the other groups, the number was not sufficient to give the best ones opportunity to score their maximum, and, if more characters had been used, the better subjects in each of these groups would undoubtedly have learned some of them, in addition to those recorded for them by the tests as administered. In the reproduction task the conditions were much the same. The 48 ideas were soon fairly well learned by most of the bright 9 and 12-year groups, who accordingly became more and more alike. At the same time the number or difficulty of the 48 ideas was sufficient to give the best of the dull 9 group a chance to improve considerably throughout the five tests of the series, but the poorest made very low scores.

In these tasks, then, it appears that the limits of the tasks limited the improvement of the best in the bright 9 and the twelve-year-old groups much more than they did the achievement of the best in the dull nine-year-old group.

The nature of the drawing game is such that it would be expected to produce irregularity in variation. Steps increase in difficulty with great irregularity. The larger numbers are, on the whole, more difficult than the smaller, but the check steps are easier than the first trials. The coefficients bear out these probable irregularities, since it would be expected that greater difficulty would produce differences in ability more pronouncedly than lesser difficulty.

The differences in variation found in the mixed series, formboard, and star time remain to be explained. In each of these the task is a fixed one, as in shorthand and reproduction, but the measure of improvement is the time required to master the task. Hence, the effect of the amount of material is shown in the measures of accomplishment.

In the mixed series, dull 9 and perhaps bright 9 show an increase in variability. In all other cases in these task records, decrease in variability is indicated. It may be that the difficulty of fitting the two sequences together in the mixed series was so great for the younger subjects for all nine trials of the task that the best in each of the dull 9 and bright 9 groups were not cut down in their scores, as apparently happened with the other groups. For the other groups in the mixed series, and for all in the formboard and star time, the tasks prominently required gross muscular movements—writing, handling blocks, tracing with a pencil. Past experiences had brought these responses up to a comparatively high level of execution, so that reaction by each subject was very much affected by habits of speed. Possibly, too, native reaction time affects results. Perhaps reaction time of dull 9 children is slower than that of bright 9, dull 12, or bright 12. Social pressures produce much uniformity in speed in doing many things, of which writing and handling blocks may be instances. The dawdler is hurried; the quick, hurrying youngster is begged to go slow. Training and habits tend to make an individual handle a pencil in much the same way as do others in the group. Finally, the materials themselves place theoretical limits on the time required to handle them. Of all the tasks, there is not one that, theoretically or practically, can be done by human beings without taking some time. As individuals approach the lowest limits of time they will, of course, vary less and less. Familiarity with the motor elements of these tasks and the number of practices given make plausible the explanation that approach to a standard achievement for each group reduces variation.

A third tendency revealed by arrangement of tasks in rough order of greatest variability, as shown by maximum and minimum coefficients, is as follows:

| Dull 9 | | Bright 9 | | Dull 12 | | Bright 12 | |
|--------|------|----------|-------|----------|-------|-----------|-------|
| Shhd.  | 80–50 | Arith.  | 80–22 | Arith.  | 66–32 | Shhd.    | 45–17 |
| Arith. | 83–48 | Fmbd.   | 61–26 | Fmbd.   | 66–25 | Fmbd.    | 45–14 |
| Fmbd.  | 60–29 | Shhd.   | 50–23 | Shhd.   | 50–26 | Arith.   | 36–20 |
| Star   | 56–11 | Star    | 50–0  | Star    | 33–9  | Star     | 43–14 |
| Dr.G.  | 44–14 | Dr.G.   | 27–15 | M.S.    | 39–18 | M.S.     | 23–15 |
| Repr.  | 46–26 | Repr.   | 25–7  | Dr.G.   | 28–12 | Dr.G.    | 23–10 |
| M.S.   | 31–16 | M.S.    | 20–7  | Repr.   | 27–10 | Repr.    | 17–6  |

Shhd. = Shorthand.  Arith. = Arithmetic.  Fmbd. = Formboard.  Star. = Star Time.  Dr.G. = Drawing game.  Repr. = Reproduction.  M.S. = Mixed Series.

The order is strikingly uniform. Apparently the more novel the task the more it differentiates individuals of a group. Consideration of the formboard and the star tasks adds weight to this explanation, since in both of these tasks, which were very much unpracticed by all subjects before the experiment, preliminary practice was given as follows: in the formboard, by two trials with eyes open; in the star tracing by fifteen minutes of practice. There is very little question but that variability between individuals in these tasks would have been much greater if the preliminary practices had been omitted.

Tentative conclusions are suggested from the discussion of the variability of the data:

1. The requirements of the tasks seem to be such that the variability found in the four groups of subjects roughly groups the tasks into the same general types as do the learning curves.

2. Variability in certain tasks decreases as accomplishment approaches standard limits.

## Frequency Distributions

Total individual scores were secured by adding all test scores of the entire series, including the retention tests since they form part of the practice. Frequency tables of these scores were then made.[1] Two facts of interest are shown by these tables: considerable overlapping of scores of all groups, and wide spread of scores in each group. In every task the best subject in the dull 9 groups does better than the poorest in the bright 12. The task in which there is the least overlapping is the mixed series. The next least is reproduction. In all the other tasks the overlapping is considerable; even the arithmetic and the shorthand tasks, which appeared in the averages as having the clearest relation to brightness, showed, in arithmetic, two dull 9 scores higher than three bright 12 scores; and, in shorthand, one bright 12 at almost the median score of the dull 9, and one dull 9 above the median score for bright 12. The highest scores in arithmetic, shorthand, and reproduction are made by bright 12; in mixed series and formboard, by bright and dull 12; in star time, by dull 9. Explanations of these facts are proposed later in connection with what is seen in the psychographs.

## Psychographs

A table [2] was made which shows the scores of each subject in each task in terms of Q deviations from medians, computed when all the sixty subjects were thrown into one frequency table for each task. These deviation scores were plotted on the graphs (on pages 38 and 39) and lines drawn from point to point so as to indicate the relative position of each individual in the

[1] See footnote on page 2.
[2] *Ibid.*

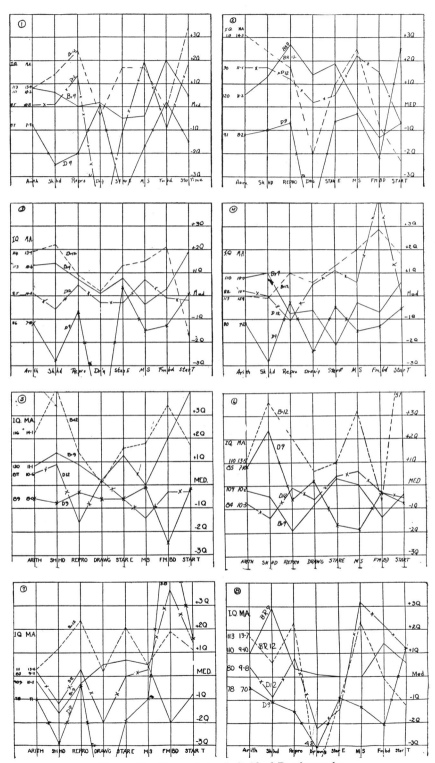

FIGURE 12. CHARTS 1-8.—Individual Psychographs

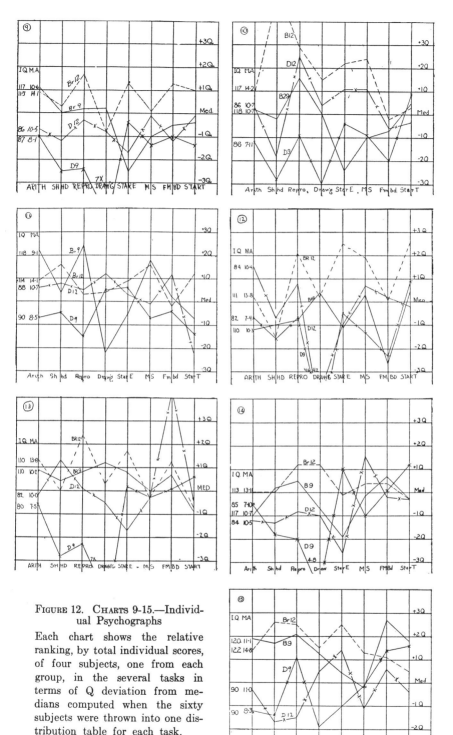

FIGURE 12. CHARTS 9-15.—Individual Psychographs

Each chart shows the relative ranking, by total individual scores, of four subjects, one from each group, in the several tasks in terms of Q deviation from medians computed when the sixty subjects were thrown into one distribution table for each task.

39

whole group. One subject from each of the groups is shown on each chart. Selection of the subjects for the charts is made on the basis of I.Q. rating, and in such a way as to pair, as nearly as possible, those subjects having the same or almost the same I.Q. Mental age is also indicated by figures at the left of each graph. This selection, of course, results in the bright 9 and dull 12 shown on each chart having nearly the same mental age.

The charts are so drawn that the tasks are in the order of the types discussed in Chapter IV. That is, reading from left to right, the tasks increase in the apparent proportion of gross motor responses demanded. The charts are numbered according to the similarity shown in the relation between subjects in arithmetic and shorthand. Beginning with Chart 1, the first seven charts show four subjects who maintain the same rank order among themselves in the two tasks. Charts 8 to 10 show those subjects of whom only one changes position in shorthand by one step; Charts 11 and 12 show those of whom only one changes position in shorthand by two steps; and Charts 13, 14 and 15 show those of whom more than one change position.

Two facts at once strike the eye as the psychographs are studied: most emphatically, the irregularity of the standing of subjects in the various tasks as indicated by the peaks, valleys, and abysmal depths of the connecting lines; less clearly, the increasing irregularity appearing in the relative positions of subjects in the tasks of Types III and IV.

Further study reveals the fact that there is no chart in which bright 12 maintains top place in all tasks. In Chart 3, bright 12 is highest except in star time, in which he is lowest. In Chart 6, he is highest in all except the formboard, in which he is next to the lowest; and in Chart 10, he is highest except in star time, where he is next to the lowest. In the twelve other charts, bright 12 loses highest positions in more than one task. In Chart 2, dull 9 is lowest in all tasks except star time, in which he is highest. In the other fourteen charts, dull 9 makes better than lowest score in two or more tasks. Referring position to the medians, it is found that bright 12 scores above the medians in every task in Charts 4, 7, and 15, while dull 9 remains below the medians in all tasks in Charts 4, 5, and 9. In the twelve other cases they go below or above the medians on one or more of the tasks.

More careful study also shows that the rank order maintained in arithmetic and shorthand by the twenty-eight subjects shown in Charts 1 to 7 is not due to their holding the same relative standing in shorthand as was held in arithmetic. Fourteen of them go higher in the shorthand than in the arithmetic and exactly the same number go lower.

What can be concluded from these facts? Clearly, that even though as few as fifteen cases smooth away variations so much that definite group characteristics appear, yet, as has always been found true, there exist very great individual differences among those composing each group.

The data give no conclusive evidence as to the causal factors for the differences. The study of special abilities and disabilities of recent years, however, has conclusively demonstrated the existence of such factors, and their presence in the work of this study was strikingly evident as the subjects went through the series of practices. For some, the multiplication facts seemed to be retained with scarcely an effort or an error, while for others none were retained, the total week's score of one or two correct being probably a matter of chance rather than of certain learning. For some, the formboard was an exciting, easy game quickly performed with scarcely a false move; others fumbled the pieces, hunted long and tediously for the places, and, having found a right place, failed to fit the piece into it and struggled for minutes elsewhere. The origin of these special characteristics will not be discussed further than to say that they may be either native, or acquired traits, or both.

A second generally accepted factor to account for differences, for which the study provides no objective evidence, is the temperamental or attitudinal natures of the subjects. It has previously been noted that in general the attitude of subjects was positive. It was early found that it was not positive to the same degree in all tasks. Subjects were asked, in an incidental way during the latter part of their work, which game they liked the best. While there was probably little careful discrimination on their part, most of them named the star tracing task. In a few cases there was quite obvious timidity toward some task. In one case, a boy who did very poorly in the formboard test seemed worried about it. He showed this both by his utterances and by the impatient, crude trial-and-error way he used in trying to place the pieces. Because of the unsatisfactory criteria available for determining emotional attitudes or temperamental traits, no attempt was made to measure them. That they are present and violently functioning is evidenced, it is believed, by the irregularities of the psychographic curves. The origin of these differences in temperament and attitude will not be discussed further than to say that they may be either native, or acquired, or both.

A third group of factors entering into this irregularity of the individual curves are the chance ones of environment and subject status, factors for which there seem to be no dependable measures. Of the three contributing groups of elements entering into individual results this group may or may not be the most important. The writer believes that chance factors are less important than either the factor of special abilities and disabilities or temperamental factors.

Apparently, then, although averages show group characteristics, the data indicate that achievement in these tasks can be predicted only roughly for any individual on the basis of I.Q., chronological age, and mental age.

# CHAPTER VI

## RESULTS: MINOR QUESTIONS

### Errors

How do the groups compare in regard to correctness of learning as indicated by errors?

Table 6 gives the average number of errors for tests and trials in arithmetic, shorthand, mixed series, and formboard tasks. Errors in star tracing are considered in Chapter IV; errors in the drawing game are found in the score used in the measure for that task, since trials in which errors were made are counted in the cumulative scores; and errors in the reproduction task will be discussed at the close of this section.

Table 6 shows that the total number of errors decreases in the mixed series and formboard tasks according to age and I.Q., the dull nine-year-old group having the greatest number in each, the bright 9 next, dull 12 third, and the bright 12 group the lowest number. In arithmetic and shorthand, however, the bright nine-year-old group has the best record of all groups, the order from most to fewest errors being dull 9, dull 12, bright 12, and bright 9.

It is difficult to find a convincing explanation for the good standing of the bright 9 group in arithmetic and shorthand. It is not due to one or more very poor bright 12 subjects making excessive numbers of errors, thus pulling the averages above what they ought to be, since, in arithmetic, the worst offender is a nine-year girl who totaled 55 errors, against 40 errors for the nearest twelve-year subject, while in shorthand each of two nine-year girls totaled more errors than any twelve-year subject. Is it because the effect of school experience is such that, while slow children are encouraged to make guesses and early learn the saving virtue of any kind of an answer over no answer at all, bright children, not being overtaxed for answers, do not build up such tendencies to guess until after several years in school? The more difficult nature of twelve-year studies, the longer oper-

TABLE 6

AVERAGE NUMBER OF ERRORS IN EACH TEST OR TRIAL IN ARITHMETIC, SHORT-
HAND, MIXED SERIES, AND FORMBOARD, BY GROUPS

| Tests | D 9 | Br 9 | D 12 | Br 12 | D 9 | Br 9 | D 12 | Br 12 |
|---|---|---|---|---|---|---|---|---|
| | | *Arithmetic* | | | | *Shorthand* | | |
| 1 | 2.6 | 2.1 | 2.8 | 2.8 | 4.7 | 3.3 | 4.1 | 3.5 |
| 2 | 3.1 | 2.6 | 3.4 | 3.1 | 6.0 | 2.9 | 3.3 | 3.1 |
| 3 | 3.9 | 2.1 | 3.2 | 2.2 | 5.2 | 2.7 | 4.1 | 3.5 |
| 4 | 5.3 | 1.5 | 3.7 | 1.7 | 5.7 | 2.6 | 3.3 | 3.3 |
| 5 | 4.5 | 1.4 | 4.0 | 2.2 | 5.9 | 3.1 | 4.3 | 3.2 |
| R | 3.9 | 1.3 | 3.5 | 2.0 | 5.8 | 2.2 | 3.6 | 3.2 |
| 6 | 4.2 | 1.6 | 3.3 | 1.7 | 5.7 | 2.8 | 4.2 | 2.9 |
| R | 4.3 | 1.4 | 3.4 | 2.3 | 5.7 | 2.2 | 4.0 | 2.7 |
| 7 | 4.7 | 1.6 | 3.4 | 1.4 | 5.8 | 2.8 | 4.1 | 3.6 |
| Total | 36.5 | 15.6 | 30.7 | 19.2 | 50.5 | 24.6 | 35.0 | 29.0 |

| Trials | | *Mixed Series* | | | | *Formboard* | | |
|---|---|---|---|---|---|---|---|---|
| 1 | 5.5 | 4.0 | 2.7 | 2.7 | 15.4 | 11.4 | 12.9 | 9.5 |
| 2 | 4.9 | 4.0 | 3.5 | 2.0 | 17.1 | 17.9 | 11.9 | 11.6 |
| 3 | 5.3 | 2.5 | 3.1 | 1.7 | 13.2 | 11.2 | 11.9 | 9.7 |
| 4 | 4.4 | 2.9 | 3.1 | 1.8 | 14.3 | 17.4 | 13.0 | 9.7 |
| 5 | 4.9 | 2.5 | 2.9 | 1.5 | 16.8 | 8.3 | 9.7 | 7.3 |
| 6 | 3.5 | 4.3 | 1.8 | 1.9 | 11.7 | 14.5 | 8.2 | 5.6 |
| 7 | 3.9 | 2.8 | 2.7 | 1.8 | 8.1 | 9.2 | 9.1 | 6.7 |
| 8 | 3.3 | 3.3 | 2.7 | .7 | 8.4 | 7.6 | 6.1 | 5.1 |
| 9 | 3.7 | 3.4 | 2.2 | 1.5 | 4.9 | 5.8 | 4.2 | 5.7 |
| 10 | | | | | 6.1 | 7.1 | 7.2 | 4.5 |
| 11 | | | | | 4.6 | 3.1 | 6.5 | 3.0 |
| 12 | | | | | 4.7 | 3.6 | 4.9 | 1.8 |
| Total | 39.4 | 29.7 | 24.7 | 15.6 | 125.3 | 117.1 | 105.6 | 80.2 |

ation of pressure to maintain a good record, and experience which
has shown the frequent gain from bluffing when not sure, may
have developed such a disposition in older bright children not
apparent when they were younger.

In these two tasks, then, arithmetic and shorthand, there appears the same general order of excellence for the groups that
was shown in Chapter IV for amount of work done—except for
the bright 9, which has a slightly better gross score record than
the bright 12.

Analysis of the mixed series and formboard tasks given in
Chapter IV indicated that important elements of the responses
demanded by them were gross muscular movements. The correct responses were already known, but were so involved in new

situations that it was difficult to get the right responses when wanted, and easy to get wrong responses. Previous consideration of the factor of gross muscular movement in accomplishment of a task suggested that age or physical maturity contributed toward good scores. By the same reasoning it could logically be advanced that physical maturity would operate to make for greater accuracy of work in older subjects. The general nature

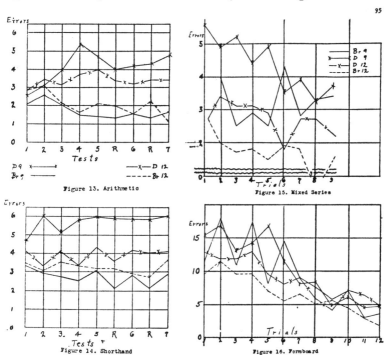

Figure 13. Arithmetic

Figure 15. Mixed Series

Figure 14. Shorthand

Figure 16. Formboard

FIGURES 13 TO 16. Comparative Rates of Improvement.

of the responses demanded by the two tasks seems to explain the likeness of the error counts shown in the performance by the groups of this experiment.

Comparative rate of improvement in accuracy of work is indicated in the charts of Figures 13 to 16, inclusive, which show the curves of the averages.[1] The two types of tasks show very different tendencies in this respect. In shorthand and arithmetic there seems to be a tendency for both dull groups to increase the num-

[1] See footnote on page 21.

ber of errors and for both bright groups to decrease theirs, and, in the mixed series and formboard, for all groups to decrease at relatively the same rate. The tasks are, therefore, again grouped in this respect, as in Chapter IV, according, it seems, to the proportion of gross muscular movement entering into the task.

It will be recalled at this point that star errors showed an order from best to poorest of bright 12, dull 12 and bright 9 together, and dull 9. It was desired to secure, if possible, some impression of relative accuracy in the reproduction task, grouped with star errors as in Chapter IV. In the administration of this task, a check list was used, on which correct ideas were checked, and, as far as possible, incorrect or correct ideas unusually worded, noted. These notes have been studied for each subject and the total number of clearly erroneous ideas counted. As gross figures, they show nothing of value, because, obviously, the dull child who may have given but six or ten ideas would not have as many wrong ones as the bright child who may have elaborated somewhat imaginatively in reproducing thirty-five or forty correct ideas. Omissions plus errors would also fail to show anything significant, since the few total errors of dull children would be fairly absorbed by the huge total of omissions, resulting in differences practically the same as omissions only, which would really be but the reverse of the number of correct ideas remembered.

Therefore, in order to furnish a comparable term which would bear a relation both to errors and to number of correct ideas, percentages of the former in terms of the latter were computed. The following shows the data and the computation of the percentages:

PER CENT OF ERRORS IN REPRODUCTION BY GROUPS

|  | Dull 9 | Bright 9 | Dull 12 | Bright 12 |
|---|---|---|---|---|
| Number of Correct Ideas ......... | 1503 | 2732 | 2658 | 3560 |
| Number of Errors ............... | 219 | 239 | 275 | 201 |
| Percentage of Errors ............ | 14.0 | 8.8 | 10.3 | 5.6 |

The figures show that dull 12 has a smaller total of correct ideas but more errors than bright 9, that bright 12 has more correct ideas and fewer errors than dull 12, and that dull 9 has considerably fewer correct ideas and almost as many errors as bright 9. The order from least to greatest per cent is: bright 12, bright 9, dull 12, and dull 9. The difference between bright 9 and dull 12 is not quite half as much as that between dull 9 and dull 12, or bright 9 and bright 12. Apparently accuracy of reproduction, requiring both memory of ideas and expression of them, arranged the groups much as does the amount of reproduction, but with more difference between bright 9 and dull 12.

CONCLUSION [1]

As measured by errors, the arithmetic, shorthand, reproduction, mixed series, formboard, and star tasks fall into the same types as when they were measured by amount of work. Apparently the proportion of gross muscular movement required by different tasks results in greater accuracy of work for older, more fully physically developed children, while tasks like the arithmetic and shorthand, in which there is a minimum of gross muscular movement and elements of greater novelty, show greater accuracy by children whose Binet rating is higher.

[1] Study was made of retention over twenty-four hours, of improvement, and of sex differences, but inasmuch as the findings were entirely negative discussion of these points is omitted in the publication of this study. The data on these points and brief discussion of them are on file with the registrar of Teachers College, Columbia University, and may be found there.

# CHAPTER VII

## SUMMARY AND CONCLUSIONS

### SUMMARY

1. Averages, learning curves, variability, and errors indicate that gross muscular movement is a determining variable in the achievement of four selected groups of children in their performance on seven practiced learning tasks of varied types.

2. There is evidence that, other things being about the same, the more novel the task, the more variable is the performance by the four groups.

3. Individual variation in all tasks is great.

### CONCLUSIONS

1. The study emphasizes the important effects of the factors of physical maturity, mental maturity, and brightness of subjects in their performance on a variety of tasks differing roughly from chiefly gross motor movement to chiefly mental responses, and involving elements ranging from the fairly familiar to the novel.

2. It presents evidence that, on the average, selection of children by the Binet test (1) fairly well assures the quality of performance on certain tasks requiring responses of like character, viz., largely mental; and (2) gives less and less assurance of the quality of performance on other tasks requiring greater and greater proportions of gross muscular responses.

3. It further presents evidence that, for individuals, selection by the Binet test gives only slight assurance of the quality of performance on any kind of task, but, in work involving a greater proportion of gross muscular movement, the prediction is more uncertain than in work that is largely mental.

In other words, the nature of the responses required in the performance of a task is involved, along with the age, brightness, and physical maturity of the individual, as determiners of the results achieved.

48

4. Other factors than the proportion of gross muscular movement involved in the responses undoubtedly enter into the quality of performance. The data seem to show that something, which is, perhaps, included under the general term "novelty," affects results in proportion as it enters into the tasks which are not fairly well determined by the more effective factors included under the category of gross muscular movement. It is this factor or group of factors which seems to differentiate the results in arithmetic and shorthand from those in reproduction and the drawing game.

5. The study, therefore, suggests the practical value of analysis of typical learning tasks to reveal the nature of responses involved and the economical location of their learning in the development of young people.

6. There does not seem to be any ability to learn in the sense of a common factor.

7. Differences in ability to learn various responses are differences in degree, not in kind. But so many functions are involved in practical experiences of life that, for these groups, separated in age by 3 years and in brightness by 30 I.Q. points, ability to learn in general is characterized, for all practical purposes, by differences in kind. Brighter individuals have that kind of ability which makes economical progress in work requiring a small proportion of gross motor movement. Dull individuals have that kind of ability which makes economical progress in work requiring a large proportion of gross muscular movement.

# ANNOTATED BIBLIOGRAPHY

No attempt is made to give citation of the entire literature in the field of the experimental study of differences in the performance or character of individuals or groups of different levels of imputed intelligence, or of differences in tasks performed by various types of subjects. Most of the experimentation in this field has been very tentative, due to meager sampling of groups and tasks and unreliable criteria, or both. The references in this bibliography are representative of the investigations experimentally made in this field. As far as the writer has been able to find, all of the very few studies comparing the performance in learning situations of children of different known Binet rating have been included.

ABELSON, A. R. "The Measurement of Mental Ability of 'Backward Children." *British Journal of Psychology*, Vol. 5, p. 268, 1911.
Found increasing coefficients of correlations with practice on mental tests of probably a difficult nature.

BAGLEY, W. C. "Mental and Motor Correlation." *American Journal of Psychology*, Vol. 12, p. 193, 1900.
From experimental data obtained by the performance of 119 school children, concluded that there was an inverse relation between motor and mental ability, but with numerous exceptions.

BOLTON, T. L. "The Relation of Motor Power to Intelligence." *American Journal of Psychology*, Vol. 14, p. 615, 1903.
From experimental data obtained by the performance of 59 "poor" children and 52 "good" children, concluded that motor power increases with age in the case of brighter children. Mind exists for the sake of movement.

BROOKS, F. D. *Changes in Mental Traits with Age.* Teachers College, Columbia University, Contributions to Education, No. 116, 1921.
172 children, grades 4–9, C.A. 9–15, were given 20 tests which were repeated after a two-year interval. The tests were grouped as requiring simpler, memory, higher, and informational functions. Concluded "gains

positive at all ages between 9 and 15. Rate of improvement is probably best represented by a straight line. . . . Correlation between gains and I.Q. low, but positive in simpler, memory, and higher functions—zero in informational."

BROWN, A. W. *The Unevenness of the Abilities of Dull and Bright Children.* Teachers College, Columbia University, Contributions to Education, No. 220, 1926.

456 boys, 10–13 M.A., were given tests in abstract, non-verbal, and mechanical abilities. The lower third, as determined by Haggerty test raw scores, were called dull, the upper third, bright. Both groups showed a great amount of unevenness, but an equal amount. Concluded that irregularity of development is not a specific characteristic of the feeble-minded.

BROWN, W. "Some Experimental Results in the Correlation of Mental Abilities." *British Journal of Psychology,* Vol. 3, 1910.

259 children and university students were given 10 tests twice each. Completion tests showed the highest correlation with intelligence estimated by teachers. Mechanical memory was next highest.

BURT, C. "Experimental Tests of General Intelligence." *British Journal of Psychology,* Vol. 3, p. 94, 1909.

43 boys were given 12 tests. Their intelligence was estimated by teachers and students. In sensori-motor and easy mental tests the correlation with intelligence was lower on the second trial than on the first, but the differences were very small. The correlation of types of tests with I.Q. were, from lowest to highest: sensory discrimination, motor ability, sensori-motor functions, association, voluntary attention. Proposes voluntary attention as the essential factor in intelligence, rather than relating factors.

CHAPMAN, J. C. *Individual Differences in Ability and Improvement and Their Correlations.* Teachers College, Columbia University, Contributions to Education, No. 63, 1914.

Practiced 22 college students in color naming, cancellation, opposites, and arithmetic. Found composite practice curves of four types: (1) rapid rise with flattening, color naming, and opposites; (2) less rapid rise, less flattening, cancellation; (3) greater rectilinearity, addition; (4) continued rapid rise, multiplication. Four random individual curves of each test showed no uniformity.

COLVIN, S. S. "Notes on Certain Aspects of Learning." *Psychological Bulletin,* Vol. 12, p. 67, 1915.

Paired 5 normal with 5 subnormal of same mental age and gave practice in cancelling a's. Found improvement with less fluctuation in every case.

DALLENBACH, K. M. "The Effect of Practice Upon Visual Apprehension in School Children, Part I." *Journal of Educational Psychology*, Vol. 5, p. 321, 1914.

29 normal and backward children, divided into good, medium, and poor observers on the basis of initial tests, practiced 76 series of exposures of various numbers, letters, and forms, over a period of 17 weeks, showed similar curves for all types of material, the poorest group making less rapid early, but more continuous later gain, than the better groups. Individual differences appeared great.

DALLENBACH, K. M. "The Effect of Practice Upon Visual Apprehension in the Feeble-Minded." *Journal of Educational Psychology*, Vol. 10, p. 61, 1919.

41 feeble-minded, 10-18 C.A., averaging 7.5 M.A., were given practically the same material as used in the 1914 study. The "feeble-minded and poorest third of the normal group continue to improve, whereas the superior and medium subjects of the normal group show a large initial increase and then a long plateau." Found a direct correlation between range of visual apprehension and mental age. Individual differences were marked, but closely correlated with mental age.

GARRETT, H. E. *Statistics in Psychology and Education.* Longmans Green, 1926.

Source of statistical formulae used in the study.

GATES, A. I. *The Psychology of Reading and Spelling, with Special Reference to Disability.* Teachers College, Columbia University, Contributions to Education, No. 129, 1922.

Differences in native ability, including striking disability, are real, according to most substantial evidence. Suggests the location of the causes to be in the enormously varying permutations and combinations of possibly a multitude of unfavorable traits.

GATES, G. S. *Individual Differences as Affected by Practice.* Columbia University, Archives of Psychology, No. 58, 1922.

Tested 23 women, college students, in color naming, tapping, adding, multiplying, and word-building, more than 20 times each test, and found that tests of higher "more intellectual" functions seem to gravitate to high negative correlations, and "motor" functions more frequently below the middle. Opposites, calculations, and multiplication "are definitely at the top. Tapping and crossing are always at the bottom and color naming is always mediocre."

HOLLINGWORTH, H. L. "Correlation of Abilities as Affected by Practice." *Journal of Educational Psychology*, Vol. 4, p. 405, 1913.

13 college subjects had 205 practices in adding, opposites, coördination, color naming, discrimination, reaction to colors, and tapping. Average correlations by rank method were positive and increased, except addition and coördination which decreased, discrimination decreased (except with tapping), coördination decreased, and tapping was irregular.

HOLLINGWORTH, L. S. *Psychology of Special Disability in Spelling.* Teachers College, Columbia University, Contributions to Education, No. 88, 1918.

Under extended experimental conditions, 15 fifth-grade children deficient in spelling but average in other subjects were studied and conclusions were drawn that disability is not a function of quality of intelligence.

HOLLINGWORTH, L. S. *Psychology of Subnormal Children.* Macmillan, 1920.

Abilities of subnormal individuals are irregular. They are below all norms, but not equally so, being nearest in physical size, strength, sensory acuity, and motor control, and farthest in abstract functions. Learning of subnormals is not the same for chronological age; it is the same for mental age.

JOHNSON, B. "Practice Effects in a Target Test, a Comparison of Groups of Varying Intelligence." *Psychological Review,* Vol. 26, p. 300, 1919.

12 female subjects in a state reformatory—3 upper level, 5 medium, 4 lower level—practiced 10 throws daily for 4 weeks. "It seems clear that a higher intelligence level makes for superiority in the target test." There was greater variability in the curves of high and low than in that of the medium group.

JONES, V. A. *Effect of Age and Experience on Tests of Intelligence.* Teachers College, Columbia University, Contributions to Education, No. 203, 1926.

Study of achievement of 487 school children in four different schools, in four intelligence tests, showed that the best sub-tests for measures of intelligence were "information," "sentence completion," "analogies," "logical selection"; and that some which ranked lowest were "visual comparison," "symbol digit," "fundamentals in arithmetic," and "picture completion." It was also found that a sub-test might rank higher at one chronological age and mental age than at another.

KUHLMANN, F. "Experimental Studies in Mental Deficiency." *American Journal of Psychology,* Vol. 15, p. 391, 1904.

3 imbeciles and 6 feeble-minded closely maintained relative ranks in target throwing and tapping during practice.

MURDOCK, K. "Rate of Improvement of Feeble-Minded as Shown by Standard Educational Tests." *Journal of Applied Psychology,* Vol. 2, 1918.

Showed that during the interval of one year feeble-minded of equal mental age failed to make as much progress as normal children in educational subject matter.

MUSCIO, B. "Motor Capacity with Special Reference to Vocational Guidance." *British Journal of Psychology,* Vol. 13, p. 157, 1922.

Tested 88 boys and girls in 12 varied motor tests and 3 mental tests. Concluded that many, but not all, mental tests correlate higher than many motor tests, hence "mental capacity" but "motor capacities," that there is no motor type, and that motor capacities are relatively independent of intelligence.

MYERS, G. C. "Some Variabilities and Correlations in Learning." *American Journal of Psychology,* Vol. 29, p. 316, 1918.

With normal school students sorting cards and fitting cubes in a box, it was found that "relative ranking of individuals of a group, working at the same task over a long period of time, tends to remain pretty much the same."

NORSWORTHY, N. *The Psychology of Mentally Deficient Children.* Columbia University, Archives of Psychology, Vol. 1, 1906.

157 defectives, 8–16 C.A. were compared with normal children in perception, memory, motor, physical, and abstract tests. Concluded that they were physically indistinguishable in muscular control, that the feeble-minded were below normal children of the same age, that in intelligence they did not form a separate species but belonged at the extreme position of some large distribution, approximating the normal curve, and that there is not an equal lack of mental ability in all directions.

ORDAHL, L. E., and ORDAHL, G. "Qualitative Differences Between Levels of Intelligence in Feeble-Minded Children." *Journal of Psycho-Asthenics,* Vol. 7, 1915.

30 subjects, 15–35 C.A. and 6, 8, and 10 M.A., were given 15 sets of experiments in visual attention, judgment of form and size, and visual motor coördination. It was found that feeble-minded improve with practice, those of higher mental age the more.

PERRIN, F. A. C. "The Learning Curves of the Analogies and the Mirror Reading Tests." *Psychological Review,* Vol. 26, p. 42, 1919.

Superior individuals ranked higher in the mirror test at first; in the analogies they ranked higher at the last. The inferior stood in just the reverse order. Results were thought to be "due to the nature of the tests themselves, rather than to the personnel of the practicing groups."

PETERSEN, A. M., and DOLL, E. A. "Sensory Discrimination in Normal and Feeble-Minded Children." *Training School Bulletin,* Vol. 11, Nos. 7 and 8, 1914.

203 feeble-minded and 262 normal children were tested in discrimination of weights. Concluded "the sensory capacity of defectives in muscle sense is not noticeably below normal." The discrimination of defectives is slightly below that of normals of the same mental age, because of psychological rather than sensory factors. Found positive correlation with intelligence, not with chronological age alone.

PETERSON, J. C. "The Higher Mental Processes in Learning." *Psychological Monographs,* Vol. 28, No. 129, 1920.

Study was made of a problem game (similar to the drawing game of this study) played by 45 adult subjects under certain fixed conditions varied as progress in learning was made. Analysis of the processes involved was attempted.

RACE, H. V. *Improvability: Its Correlations and Its Relations to Initial and General Ability.* Teachers College, Columbia University, Contributions to Education, No. 124, 1922.

95 junior and senior college students, 43 third- and fourth-grade children above 124 I.Q., and 172 average children in grades four, five, and seven, practiced addition, multiplication, cancellation, language completion, reasoning in history, and Thorndike intelligence examinations. Correlations corrected for attenuation were computed. Concluded that "improvability or learning seems to be specialized, rather than unitary." Higher levels produced greater improvement. Lower levels learned at a slower rate, the higher at a faster rate. Improvability correlates with I.Q.

RUCH, G. M. "The Influence of the Factor of Intelligence on the Form of the Learning Curve." *Psychological Monographs,* Vol. 34, No. 160, 1925.

50-65 children of mental ages 8-18, chronological age mode of 14, and I.Q. Binet range of 75 points practiced 10 days on three tests: (1) card sorting, (2) code substitution, (3) abstract relations. Each test seemed to be of a distinct type. In card sorting the correlation of day 1 with day 10 scores was lowest of the three, the coefficient of variation was lowest and most constant, and the learning curves converged. The relations test showed highest correlation between first and last day scores, greatest variability, and diverging learning curves. The code test stood between the other two, the curves remaining practically parallel. Concluded that learning curves vary with the type of mental function practiced, and according to the mental abilities of the learners.

SIMPSON, B. R.  *Correlations of Mental Abilities.* Teachers College, Columbia University, Contributions to Education, No. 53, 1912.

17 "good" adults and 29 "poor" adults were given 15 tests resulting in correlations of the order from low to high: sensory discrimination, motor control, quickness and accuracy of perception, memory and association, and selective thinking.

STARCH, D.  *Educational Psychology,* Macmillan, 1919.

Gives the description of the star mirror drawing experiment used in this study, page 30.

TERMAN, L. M.  "Genius and Stupidity, a Study of Some of the Intellectual Processes of Seven 'Bright' and Seven 'Stupid' Boys." *Pedagogical Seminary,* Vol. 13, p. 307, 1906.

Bright subjects were much superior to stupid when compared in higher mental processes such as puzzles, inventions, etc., the least difference being in invention.

WOODROW, H.  "Practice and Transference in Normal and Feeble-Minded Children." *Journal of Educational Psychology,* Vol. 8, p. 85, 1917.

20 feeble-minded and 16 normal children of nearly the same mental age and initial ability sorted marked gun wads on 13 days. It was found "impossible to establish any significant differences in improvability." In transference to sorting sticks and pegs, the groups were "practically the same; in cancellation, normal children were slightly better." In general, concluded there was no significant difference.

WYATT, S.  "The Quantitative Investigation of Higher Mental Processes." *British Journal of Psychology,* Vol. 6, 1913.

75 children were given 15 tests, twice each. Found that analogies and completion correlated highest with intelligence, as estimated by teachers, memory correlated next highest.